THE WONDERS OF OUR WORLD

Mountains

Neil Morris

CRABTREE PUBLISHING COMPANY

www.crabtreebooks.com

The Wonders of our World

Crabtree Publishing Company

Author: Neil Morris
Managing editor: Peter Sackett
Editors: Ting Morris & David Schimpky
Designer: Richard Rowan
Production manager: Graham Darlow
Picture research: Lis Sackett

Picture Credits:
Artists: Martin Camm, Ruth Lindsay
Maps: European Map Graphics Ltd
Photographs: John Cleare 25 (right). Colorific 28 (bottom).
Genesis Space Photo Library 25 (left); Robert Harding Picture
Library 3, 4 (bottom), 6 (bottom), 7 (bottom), 8 (top), 10 (top),
12 (top), 13, 14 (top), 16, 22 (bottom). Caroline Jones 15.
John Noble 29 (right). Telegraph Colour Library 18 (bottom),
28 (top). Topham Picturepoint 4 (top), 5 (bottom), 6 (top)
10 (bottom), 12 (bottom), 14 (bottom), 17, 18 (top), 22 (top),
23 (top), 24 (top), 26, 27.

Crabtree Publishing Company

www.crabtreebooks.com   1-800-387-7650

Cataloging-in-publication data

Morris, Neil
　　　　Mountains
p. cm. — (The Wonders of our world)
Includes index.
ISBN 0-86505-829-6 (library bound) ISBN 0-86505-841-5 (pbk).
This book looks at the natural characteristics and ecology of
mountains.
1. Mountains—Juvenile literature. 2. Mountain ecology—
Juvenile literature. I. Title. II. Series: Morris, Neil. Wonders
of our world.

GB512.M66 1995   j508.3134 20   LC 95-23442 CIP

**Published in
the United States**
PMB 16A
350 Fifth Ave.
Suite 3308
New York, NY
10118

**Published
in Canada**
616 Welland Ave.,
St. Catharines,
Ontario, Canada
L2M 5V6

**Published in the
United Kingdom**
73 Lime Walk
Headington
Oxford
0X3 7AD
United Kingdom

**Published
in Australia**
386 Mt. Alexander Rd.,
Ascot Vale (Melbourne)
V1C 3032

CONTENTS

WHAT ARE MOUNTAINS?

MOUNTAINS ARE parts of the earth's surface that stand high above their surroundings. They are like bumps on the world's globe. Some are steep and form high, sharp peaks. Other, lower mountains are more gentle and rounded. Smaller rises are usually called hills. Most mountains are at least 300 meters (980 feet) high.

Mountains are often joined together in a series, or range. When ranges are grouped together, they are called a chain. The longest and highest ranges, such as the Andes and the Himalayas, form huge mountain systems.

SNOW IN AFRICA

AT a height of 5895 meters (19,340 feet) Mount Kilimanjaro, in Tanzania, is the highest mountain in Africa. At the top, it is cold enough for snow to stay all year round, even though this single peak is near the equator.

JAGGED PEAKS

The Dolomites, in northeastern Italy, are made up of steep-sided rocky peaks. The highest peak, Marmolada, rises to 3342 meters (10,965 feet). This range forms part of a chain called the Alps.

UP IN THE CLOUDS

Alaska's Mount McKinley, also called Denali, is the highest point in North America. It is part of the Alaska Range and rises to 6198 meters (20,335 feet). High peaks are very often up in the clouds or even above them. In winter, blizzards blow around the mountaintops.

THE GREAT RANGES

THE TWO longest mountain ranges in the world are the Andes, in South America, and the Rockies, in North America. Together they form a great mountain system known as the Cordilleras. This system runs near the Pacific coasts of both continents.

The Alpine-Himalayan system is a curving series of ranges that runs across Europe and Asia. At its eastern end lie the world's highest mountains, including the highest of all, Mount Everest.

ANDES

The world's longest mountain range stretches for 7200 kilometers (4475 miles). Many rivers, including the Urubamba River, begin high in the Peruvian Andes.

ROCKIES

THE Rocky Mountains are 4800 kilometers (2980 miles) long. They run from northwestern Canada to the southwestern United States. These rocky peaks in Jasper National Park, Alberta, overlook beautiful Medicine Lake.

FAMOUS RANGES

The map shows where some of the world's best-known mountain ranges are located. They are spread across all the continents.

1. Alaska Range
2. Rockies
3. Appalachians
4. Andes
5. Alps
6. Pyrenees
7. Atlas Mountains
8. Urals
9. Caucasus
10. Tien Shan
11. Himalayas
12. Great Dividing Range

HIMALAYAS

The world's highest mountain range stretches across the border between India and Tibet, through the small kingdoms of Bhutan and Nepal, to northern Pakistan. The Annapurna peaks (right) rise to 8091 meters (26,545 feet).

HOW DO MOUNTAINS FORM?

THERE ARE various kinds of mountains. They are created in different ways. All, however, are formed by the movement of rocks in the earth's surface.

The earth's rocky outer layer is called its crust. It is made up of huge pieces called plates, which fit together like a giant jigsaw puzzle. As plates push against each other, they buckle at the edges and push mountains up. If the crust cracks, it has the same effect. Sometimes molten rock bursts through the crust to make a volcano.

VOLCANIC MOUNTAINS
A volcano erupts when molten rock forces its way through a crack in the earth's crust. Over time, cooled lava and ash build a higher mountain.

DIFFERENT MOUNTAINS

FOLD mountains are formed when one plate slides under another. The Andes, Rockies, and Himalayas were all made in this way. Block mountains are created when the earth's crust cracks and a chunk of land is pushed up.

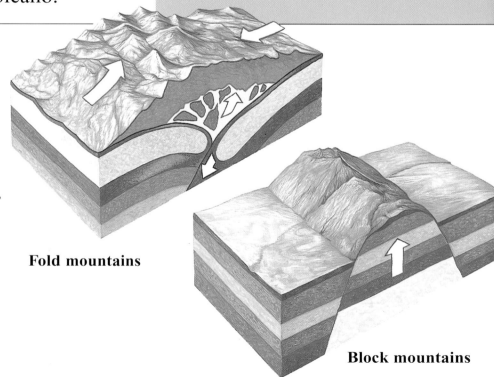

Fold mountains

Block mountains

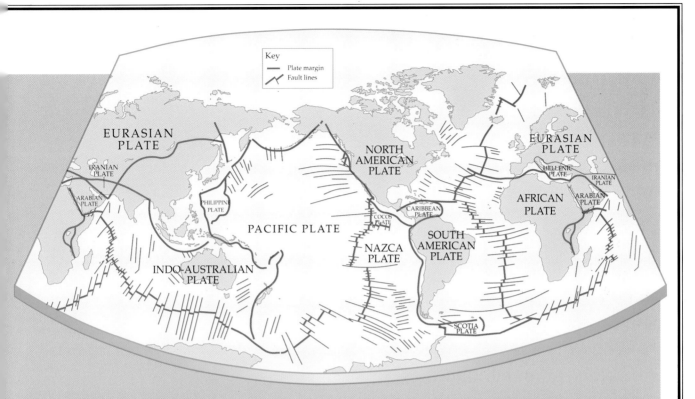

THE EARTH'S PLATES

This map shows the world's major plates. They move a very tiny distance each year, changing the shape of continents and creating volcanoes and mountain ranges.

There are mountain ranges on the ocean floor, too. They form at the edge of plates and are called ridges. The longest series of ridges runs under the sea for 65,000 kilometers (40,400 miles).

Dome mountains form when the top layers of the earth's crust are pushed up by molten rock underneath. The molten rock, called magma, turns solid again beneath the bulging surface. If the magma breaks through the crust, it is called a volcano. The volcano spews out molten rock.

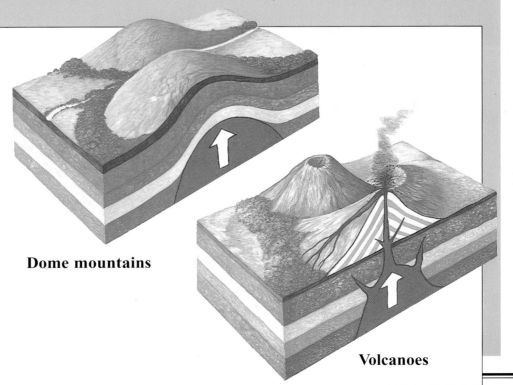

Dome mountains

Volcanoes

FOLDS AND FAULTS

THE EARTH'S plates are made up of layers of rock, called strata. As the plates move, the strata are pushed and bent into folds. The movement is very slight, but it exerts great force over millions of years. Ranges of folded mountains, such as the Himalayas, are still being pushed up in this way.

When the strata are pushed and folded so much that they cannot bend any more, they break and form a crack called a fault. The world's mountains are made of folds and faults.

SAN ANDREAS FAULT

In California, the Pacific and North American plates meet. They form the San Andreas Fault, where the two plates slide past each other, moving about 5 centimeters (2 inches) every year. Transform faults often cause earthquakes.

STRATA

WE CAN often see evidence of folding rocks in mountains. In this part of the Apennines range in Italy, the strata are exposed and show how they have been folded into wavy lines.

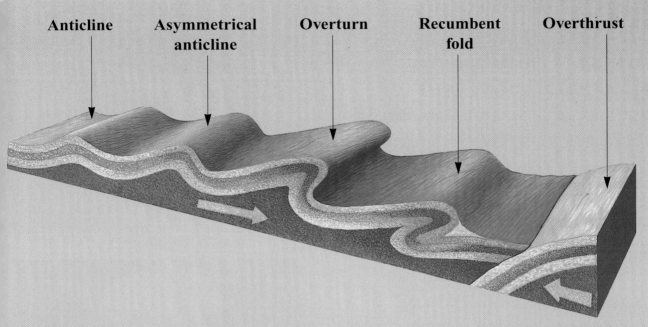

Anticline · Asymmetrical anticline · Overturn · Recumbent fold · Overthrust

FOLDING LAYERS

As strata are pushed and folded, they form upward bumps called anticlines. Some are asymmetrical, which means they are steeper on one side than the other.

As the strata get more compressed, they begin to turn over. They may then form a pleat, called a recumbent fold. Sometimes the strata break and move over each other in an overthrust.

FAULT TYPES

A NORMAL fault is caused when rocks are stretched apart. When they are pushed together, they may create a reverse or thrust fault. Plates slide past each other in a transform fault.

Normal

Transform

Reverse

Thrust

ROCKS

MOUNTAINS are made of many different rocks, but there are three basic types of rock in the earth's crust. Igneous (or "fiery") rocks form when magma from inside the earth cools and hardens. When igneous rock fragments are worn away by the weather, the fragments, or sediment, usually settle on a seabed. The sediment builds layers of sedimentary rock. Great pressure or heat can change sedimentary and igneous rocks into metamorphic rock.

SEDIMENTARY

THE sediment that makes up all sedimentary rocks contains fragments of dead plants and animals, as well as igneous rocks. Limestone was used by the ancient Egyptians to construct the Step Pyramid (left, above). Sandstone and chalk (left, below) are also sedimentary rocks.

IGNEOUS

WHEN magma hardens on the surface of the earth, it forms rocks such as basalt. These pillars of basalt rock (far left) are in Algeria. Granite (left, lying in the desert) is a very hard igneous rock that forms underground.

METAMORPHIC

Changes that make metamorphic rocks also create gemstones. Jade comes from two rocks: jadeite and nephrite. It was used to make this ancient Chinese burial suit (right). Marble forms when limestone is heated and squeezed. White marble is often used for sculpture and decoration (below).

WEARING AWAY

V ERY OLD mountain ranges, such as the Appalachians, in the eastern United States, and the Urals, in Russia, were pushed up more than 250 million years ago. Their peaks are now much lower than they once were because they have been worn down by erosion.

As soon as a mountain forms, it is attacked by wind, rain, and ice, as well as changes in temperature. Most erosion is caused by streams and rivers, which scrape away at the rock.

WATER EROSION

S TREAMS and young rivers near their source, like this stream in the Rocky Mountains, travel quickly down mountain slopes. They carry grit and rocks with them.

ROCK GLACIER

A stream of small rock fragments moves slowly down Rainbow Mountain in Alaska. Rock glaciers are similar to ice glaciers. The rock fragments are often held together with ice, and the glacier moves as the ice slowly melts.

HIGHLANDS

IN EUROPE, the Scottish Highlands (above) and the Scandinavian Range are also old mountain chains.

Their slopes are much more gentle and rounded than they once were. They have been worn down by glaciers and other forms of erosion over millions of years.

BLUE MOUNTAINS

Part of Australia's Great Dividing Range, few of these old mountains are over 1000 meters (3280 feet) high. Eucalyptus trees, which cover the lower slopes, release a fine blue mist of oil, giving these mountains their name.

MOUNTAIN WEATHER

HIGH MOUNTAIN ranges form barriers across the land. All over the world, heavy rainfall is found on the windward slopes of mountains —slopes that have the wind blowing towards them. The leeward side of the mountains, where the wind is blowing away, receives much less rain.

Air cools as it rises, so the higher the mountain, the colder the weather at its peak. This is why high peaks are covered in snow, even in the hottest parts of the world.

RAIN SHADOW

WATER evaporates and forms clouds. As the clouds pass over mountains, rain falls. When they reach the other side, they have lost most of their water. The dry, far side is in a rain shadow.

Evaporation

Evaporation

Rain

Rain shadow

MOUNTAIN WINDS

AS wind flows down mountain slopes, it warms very quickly. The warm, dry föhn wind blows from the Alps. It can cause avalanches (left) and change alpine weather very quickly. On the eastern slopes of the Rockies, similar winds are called chinooks.

CLIMATE IN THE HIGH ANDES

Mountain climates change according to altitude. In the Andes, below about 1000 meters (3280 feet), the climate is tropical, and there are many dense rain forests. Higher up the weather grows much cooler. The Andes are at their widest in Bolivia. In the eastern part (above), deep valleys called yungas have been cut by rivers. The valleys have a mild climate, and are good for farming.

The Andean highlands of Peru (left) are rugged, and rain falls only in the warm summer months. Local people farm in the valleys.

PLANT LIFE

HIGH UP on mountains, the air has little oxygen. A cold wind is usually blowing. The soil is thin and stony, so trees and bushes have tough roots that can force their way into rocky cracks. The roots act as an anchor against the wind.

The upper limit of tree growth is called the tree line. Above this level, only tough grasses and low flowering plants grow. Higher still there are just mosses and lichens. At the peaks there are no plants, just bare rocks, snow, and ice.

ALPINE FLOWERS
These alpine buttercups are growing on a stony mountainside. Mountain plants have thread-like roots that spread out to find cracks in rocks.

IN THE HIMALAYAS

MANY plants, including rhododendrons, bloom in the lower hills of the Himalayas. Above about 2000 meters (6560 feet), forests are filled with evergreen trees. The tree line is at about 3500 meters (11,500 feet).

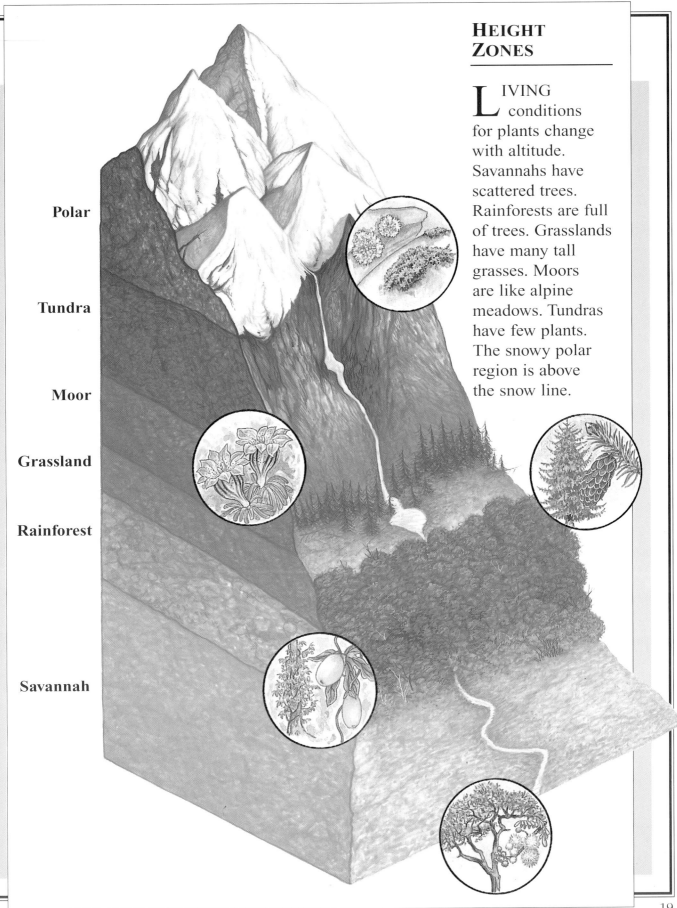

HEIGHT ZONES

Polar

Tundra

Moor

Grassland

Rainforest

Savannah

L IVING conditions for plants change with altitude. Savannahs have scattered trees. Rainforests are full of trees. Grasslands have many tall grasses. Moors are like alpine meadows. Tundras have few plants. The snowy polar region is above the snow line.

ANIMALS

MOUNTAIN animals have adapted to life in a harsh, rugged environment. Some, such as the yak, have thick coats to keep them warm. A few of these large shaggy oxen live at altitudes of up to 6000 meters (19,700 feet) in the Himalayas, but so many have been hunted that they are nearly extinct. Other animals like to sleep through the winter months. Bears that live in forests on the lower slopes use a cave for their winter sleep.

MOUNTAIN LION

Mountain lions, also called pumas or cougars, live in a variety of habitats—even high mountain areas. They have been found at altitudes of over 4000 meters (13,100 feet) in the Rockies. They will eat almost any prey, from hares to deer. They live in parts of North America and throughout much of South America.

MOUNTAIN GOAT

THE male ibex has long horns, which it sometimes uses to fight off rivals. In the high mountains of the Alps and the Himalayas, the sure-footed ibex climbs along rocky crags. It moves down to lower slopes in winter.

ALL OVER THE WORLD

These animals all live in mountain regions, but in very different parts of the world. Most move to lower altitudes in winter.

1. Andean Condor
2. Snow Leopard
3. Chamois
4. Brown Bear
5. Giant Panda
6. Salmon
7. Vulture
8. Mountain Gorilla
9. Alpine marmot
10. Pronghorn

MOUNTAIN PEOPLES

SCIENTISTS have found that, just like plants and animals, people have adapted specially to life at high altitudes. High mountain dwellers have a rich supply of red cells in their blood. This allows their bodies to take more oxygen from the air. People used to living at lower altitudes feel dizzy and short of breath if they climb much above 3000 meters (9840 feet). Yet, the capital of Bolivia, La Paz, lies in the Andes at 3630 meters (11,900 feet), and over a million people live there.

HIMALAYAN SHEPHERD
A young shepherd leads his herd of goats and sheep along a valley track in Nepal. Many people in this Himalayan kingdom are farmers. The Sherpas are used to life in the high mountains.

ON LAKE TITICACA
This lake lies in the Andes, on the border between Peru and Bolivia. It is the highest navigable lake in the world, and its shores are home to the Aymara people. They traditionally live by farming and fishing in the lake from reed boats.

ALPINE VILLAGE

LIFE IN this alpine village on the River Inn, in eastern Switzerland, changes dramatically from summer to winter. In summer, farmers graze their cattle on the rich mountain meadows.

The Swiss Alps are a favorite region for walkers and more serious climbers.

When the first snows cover the pastures, the farmers bring their cattle down to live in cow-sheds. Soon, the village fills with visitors who have come to ski the mountainsides.

ON TOP OF THE WORLD

MOST OF the world's highest mountains are in the Himalayas. This includes the highest of them all, Mount Everest, which lies on the border between the kingdom of Nepal and Tibet, a self-governing province of China. The mountain was named after a British Surveyor General, George Everest. Tibetans call the mountain Qomolongma, which means "goddess mother of the world." Recent satellite surveys have measured Everest at 8863 meters (29,078 feet).

MOUNTAIN MAPPING

THE MAP (left) shows where Mount Everest is. It was first calculated to be the highest mountain in the world in 1852, during a survey of India. In more recent years, the Himalayas have been surveyed, photographed, and mapped from planes and even satellites.

Photographs from above, such as the one on the right, are turned into side views by special computer programs. They provide us with a picture that is impossible to see or photograph from the ground. Most modern maps are made using computer images.

CONQUEST OF EVEREST

THIS photograph was the first taken at the highest point on Earth. In 1953, Edmund Hillary, a climber from New Zealand, photographed Tenzing Norgay, a Nepalese mountaineer. The two had just become the first people to reach the summit of Mount Everest.

CLIMBING TO THE TOP

Since that historic day in 1953, many mountaineers have climbed Everest. In 1992, 32 climbers from five expeditions all reached the summit on the same day! Mountain climbing requires good equipment and lots of teamwork. To climb this overhang (right), a member of the team had to first secure the ropes.

USING MOUNTAINS

MANY OF the world's largest metal mines are in mountain areas. Mountains have also been useful for hydroelectric projects, producing electricity from the power of rushing water.

Today, mountains all over the world are visited by millions of people. Mountain climbing, hiking, and skiing are all very popular sports. There are also adventure holidays to some very remote mountain areas, such as the Himalayas and the Andes.

ROCK CLIMBING
Climbers attach themselves to the mountain with strong ropes, just in case of a slip. They wear helmets as protection against falling rocks.

SNOWY MOUNTAINS SCHEME
Lake Eucumbene was created as part of a hydroelectric project in the Snowy Mountains of Australia. The Snowy River was dammed, filling a valley. Huge tunnels take water through the mountains to nearby farmland.

WINTER SPORTS

SKIING IS an important part of the tourist industry in many mountainous countries. There are hundreds of modern ski resorts in the United States and Canada, especially in the Rockies. In Europe, the Swiss, Austrian, French, and Italian Alps are popular destinations for skiers.

HANG-GLIDING

THIS hang-glider, sailing above Innsbruck in Austria, has a great view of the River Inn valley and the Karwendel mountains. Like birds, hang-gliders use warm air currents to stay aloft for as long as possible.

THE FUTURE

PEOPLE ARE changing the face of mountains. In many regions, mountain forests have been cut down to provide timber, to create farmland, and for building towns. This has left slopes bare and led to landslides and floods.

In other places, tourists wear away vegetation and soil as they look for mountain adventure. In the future, we must do our best to look after our mountains, so that people, animals, and plants can continue to use and enjoy them.

MOUNTAIN FOREST

Forests that cover mountains collect rainfall and release it slowly to fill rivers below. Cutting down forests can have disastrous effects on the environment.

LOGGERS

THE mountain forests of the islands of Borneo and Sumatra are being cut down for timber. Many rare animals live in these dense forests. Losing their home may mean extinction.

NATURE RESERVE

MANY of the trees in the Himalayas have been cut down by loggers. When mountain regions are changed or destroyed by people, wildlife can seldom adapt quickly enough to new conditions. This means that animals and plants can die out.

To stop this from happening, many governments have set aside nature reserves and national parks. In Nepal (right), parks have provided safe homes for endangered species of Himalayan mountain goats, deer, pheasant, and many other animals. More protected spaces are needed around the world to help save mountain wildlife.

GLOSSARY

Anticline	An upward bump in the earth's crust.
Avalanche	A large fall of snow or rocks down a mountainside.
Blizzard	Strong cold winds blowing heavy snowfall.
Chain	A group of mountain ranges.
Chinook	A warm, dry wind that blows down the Rockies.
Continent	One of the earth's seven huge land masses.
Crust	The hard outer layer of the earth.
Equator	An imaginary circle that stretches around the middle of the earth.
Erosion	The wearing away of rocks by water and wind.
Evaporate	To change from a liquid to a vapor.
Fault	A crack in the earth's crust.
Föhn	A warm, dry wind that blows down the Alps.
Fold	A bend in a layer of rock caused by plate movement.
Foothills	The lower slopes of a mountain.
Glacier	A slowly moving mass of ice, or of rock fragments in a rock glacier.
Hydroelectric	Describing electricity made from rushing water.
Igneous	Describing rocks made from lava on the earth's surface, or from cooled magma beneath it.
Lava	Molten rock that pours out of a volcano.
Magma	Hot molten rock formed beneath the earth's surface.

Metamorphic	Describing rocks changed from their original structure by great heat or pressure.
Molten	Melted; turned into liquid.
Overthrust	A fault where the rocks on the upper surface have moved over rocks on the lower surface.
Peak	The pointed top of a mountain.
Plate	A huge piece of the earth's crust; the earth's plates fit together like a giant jigsaw puzzle.
Recumbent	Describing a fold forming a pleat; doubled-back.
Reverse fault	A type of fault caused by rocks being pushed together.
Ridge	A mountain range on the ocean floor.
Savannah	Grassland with scattered bushes or trees.
Sedimentary	Describing rocks formed by fragments of igneous rock that have been deposited by water, ice, or wind.
Snow line	The altitude above which there is always snow.
Strata	Layers of rock.
Thrust fault	A type of fault caused by rocks being pushed together.
Transform fault	A fault in which blocks of rock slide past each other.
Tree line	The altitude above which no trees grow.
Tundra	A cold zone between the tree line and the snow line.
Volcano	An opening where molten rock and gas come from deep inside the earth, often forming a mountain.

INDEX

A
Alaska Range 5, 7
Alps 4, 7, 17, 20, 23, 27
Andes 4, 6, 7, 8, 17, 22, 26
Annapurna peaks 7
Apennines 10
Appalachians 7, 14
Atlas Mountains 7

B
basalt 13
blizzards 5
block mountains 8
Blue Mountains 15

C
Caucasus 7
chinooks 17
continents 7, 9
crust 8-9, 12

D
Dolomites 4
dome mountains 9

E
erosion 14-15, 28

F
faults 10, 11
föhn wind 17
fold mountains 8, 10, 11
forests 18, 28

G
granite 13
Great Dividing Range 7, 15

H
hang-gliding 27
height zones 19
Hillary, Edmund 25
Himalayas 4, 7, 8, 10, 18, 20, 22, 24, 26, 29
hydroelectric projects 26

I
ibex 20
igneous rocks 12-13

J
jade 13

L
Lake Eucumbene 26
Lake Titicaca 22
logging 28, 29

M
magma 9, 12, 13
marble 13
Marmolada 4
metamorphic rock 12, 13
mining 26
Mount Everest 6, 24-25
Mount Kilimanjaro 4
Mount McKinley 5
mountain climate 16-17
mountain formation 8-9
mountain goat *see* ibex
mountain lion 20
mountain mapping 24

N
nature reserves 29
Norgay, Tenzing 25

P
people 22-23, 26, 28, 29
plants 13, 18-19, 22, 28, 29
plates 8, 9, 10, 11
Pyrenees 7

R
Rainbow Mountain 14
ridges 9
rock climbing 25, 26
Rocky Mountains 6, 7, 8, 14, 17, 20

S
San Andreas Fault 10
sandstone 13
Scandinavian Range 15
Scottish Highlands 15
sedimentary rock 12, 13
sports 23, 26-27
strata 10, 11

T
Tien Shan 7

U
Urals 7, 14

V
volcanoes 8, 9

W
weather 16-17

Y
yak 20
yunga 17